The Values Inspired Leader™

Colin Emerson

Colin Emerson Speaker. Sydney, Australia

The Values Inspired Leader™
Copyright © 2012 Colin Emerson.

Original Copyright: Be Billion Dollar Leader
Copyright © 2007 Colin Emerson.

All rights reserved. No part of this book may be reproduced or utilised in any form or by any means, electronic or mechanical, including photocopying, recording, or by any information storage retrieval system, without permission in writing from the publisher, nor be circulated in any form of binding or cover other than that in which it is published without a similar condition being imposed on the subsequent publisher. A limited quotation up to a total of 500 words may be used for reference purposes, with credits duly assigned.

Enquiries should be addressed to:

Colin Emerson
colin@colinemersonspeaker.com

ISBN 978-1537734170

Created in Australia by
Colin Emerson Speaker
www.colinemersonspeaker.com

Printed by	Edited by
CreateSpace,	Alexander Goodman
Charleston SC	Canberra ACT

Dedicated to the most fantastic, high performing
Values Inspired sales team ever.

What a privilege it was to lead you:
Andrew W, Rhonda, Andrew J, Bruce, Simon, Ben, Dominic,
Anthony and Alison.

- Introduction -

Leadership!

Since time immemorial people of all races, creeds and social standing have followed the call of great leaders.

Nations have risen from nothing or have been conquered, seas have been sailed in voyages of discovery into the unknown or for trade, people have given their lives or been given life, ideas have been acted on and history made; all at the behest of a great leader.

King Richard I, Queen Victoria, George Washington, Abraham Lincoln, Winston Churchill, "Weary" Dunlop, Sir Arvi Parbo; these are all names synonymous with strong, positive leadership.

Conversely, acts of cruelty, deception, war, death, destruction, atrocity, famine and murder have been carried out by people following a leader who has led them on the wrong path. One only needs to recall the names of Hitler, Pol Pot, Stalin, and Jim Jones of the Jonestown mass suicide infamy to see that the charismatic qualities of a great leader can be used for ignoble purposes.

In today's world, corporations have been born and destroyed by the implementation of qualities, values and ethics endorsed by the leaders of those companies. Names like those of Richard Branson, Lee Iacocca and Bob Ansett stand out against their ethical opposites such as Bernard Ebbers, Kenneth Lay and Christopher Skase.

Thousands of words in many books have been written in order to describe the illusive characteristics that make a great leader great. Anyone wanting to know how to be a great leader can download them

i

from any online store like Amazon. Their catalogs are filled with biographies of great leaders – biographies that expose their actions, their achievements and their skill at making the impossible possible.

Yet somehow, when it comes to leadership in the workplace we seem to have missed the point of what makes a great leader great. So often the qualities that make a leader even mediocre seem lacking in business and the community in general.

The so called Global Financial Crisis is a wonderful example of what happens when the values that make great leaders great are replaced with leadership that lacks character; when leadership is driven by value rather than values.

With all this information available to us, why is that so?

One: I believe that in the corporate world we have simply confused the principles of managing people with the principles and the qualities of great leadership.

For years we have been conned into believing that good management skills equaled good leadership. *The truth is that good management skills make you a good manager.*

Two: We have confused value with values.

The day we saw people that work in businesses as "assets", something that is a bottom line cost to the business (God bless CFO's for this!), is the day we started losing sight of the true worth of the values these very same people bring, that allows this bottom line to happen.

We traded people for profits! We traded values for value.

For over 25 years I have been asked to conduct "leadership" training for national and international companies both in Australia and overseas. And, like every other trainer or executive development specialist that I know, I conducted "leadership" development programs on such topics as strategic thinking, effective communication, effective feedback and appraisal systems, personal effectiveness, staff recognition and development programs, change management, project management, staff selection and interviewing, quality customer service management, image and presentation skills and so on.

Until recently I believed, as do many others including the executives and training managers who hired me, that what we were developing was the leadership skills of their management teams. I am now part of a growing band of leadership educators who know that we were wrong.

What I have learned is that you can have excellent time management skills and not be a leader.

You can have great communication, feedback and interpersonal skills and still not be a great leader.

You can have fantastic change management, goal setting, reward and recognition and delegation skills and still only be a great manager and not a great leader.

You can have great budgeting skills and not be a great Values Inspired Leader.

True, a great leader displays all of those capabilities in varying degrees, but *leadership, truly great values inspired leadership is more about the heart and the character of a person* and not just the dry, but important, skills that are defined in nearly every text book or course that claims to be about leadership.

Don't confuse being a manager with being a leader. There is a difference. You can be one and not necessarily be the other.

Now some managers will disagree with that statement. I have often had some interesting comments made to me when I dared declare that a manager does not a leader make.

However, ask any worker in the workplace and they will surely tell you that they know of a manager who is definitely not a good leader. You may even find that these people will define someone as a great leader who does not necessarily display great management skills.

So, are leaders born or developed? The answer is – both. There are some truly gifted individuals who are born leaders. They display all of those human values that people embrace as being true greatness.

The rest of us, including myself, are left with the struggle to grow into being leaders; beyond that of just being good managers.

The *Ten Lessons in Being a Values Inspired Leader* which are defined in this book will take you to the heart of strong and ethical values inspired leadership.

These are lessons I have learned from over 35 years of being in senior management and leadership roles. They are the lessons learned from observing great leaders in both my military and civilian lives. The lessons come from researching the qualities and values that people say they look for in a great leader. They are lessons I have learned from leading high performing, high achieving, values inspired teams. They are even lessons learned from being a father of four magnificent children.

Remarkably, the *Ten Lessons in Being a Values Inspired Leader* are not complicated. In clear, plain language, these lessons are so simple that even a manager can follow them.

Like me you may not be one of the gifted born-leaders in this world but we can all take heart from the fact that these lessons are based more on attitude than on academic qualities. You can take heart that attitudes are something we each, individually control.

And, you can take heart that the values that Values Inspired Leaders integrate into their lives are the type of values any leader can display.

This means that we can all become great Values Inspired Leaders if we want to.

Colin Emerson
September 2016

– Table of Contents –

- Introduction -	i
– Definition –	
Values	11
– Lesson 1 –	
There are two types of respect	19
– Lesson 2 –	
To earn respect, I must first give respect	29
– Lesson 3 –	
I have to trust my people	41
– Lesson 4 –	
I will be promoted to my own level of incompetence, so I should employ people who make me look good!	49
– Lesson 5 –	
I work to make it work	61
– Lesson 6 –	
I am there to serve my team, not to be its servant	77
– Lesson 7 –	
A true leader is one whose boots are the first to hit the ground and are the last ones to leave!	91
– Lesson 8 –	
Be human	103
– Lesson 9 –	
A leader seeks counsel, and accepts responsibility	115
– Lesson 10 –	
A leader needs more than a vision; a leader needs to be a part of the vision	129
– A final word –	143

– Definition –
Values

– Definition –

Values

A week after the 2012 Olympic Games, I attended a conference of nearly 4,000 people.

Attendees came from over 100 counties. Some came from countries that normally don't see eye-to-eye. In fact, those countries are downright mutually hostile. Yet no-one was screened or searched for guns, explosives or potentially harmful gadgets or substances such a meeting of conflagrates could entail indeed, none were expected.

People came with different religious beliefs, or with none at all. Cultural backgrounds were as diverse as the colour of a painter's palette. There was no common educational, employment, lifestyle, income, gender or political commonality to the audience.

Business leaders, political aspirants, ordinary folk; all met in one auditorium for three days.

And yet, unlike the Olympics, which are supposed to unite the world through sport, there were no surface-to-air missile systems on roofs of buildings. There were no military or police checkpoints common with the meeting of world leaders. There were no security checks of those attending or funny men in black suits talking to their wrist while wandering around the audience.

Even rock concerts have more security!

Did that mean that everyone enjoyed a group-hug each morning of the conference and sang weird songs as they danced around the camp fire each night? No.

They were human, and like all humans they enjoyed the foibles that make us human. Yet that didn't stop them from sharing fully in this event and having fun while learning and engaging with each other.

Because what they all had in common was a set of shared values that have been ingrained into the culture of their organisation, *Toastmasters International*.

They are values that permeate the leadership, decision making, future direction and membership of the organisation.

Values that take pride of place alongside Vision and Mission statements that include integrity, dedication to excellence, service to the member and respect for the individual.

Even better, these values are actively pursued and not left as just words on a page.

Another organisation that places high precedence on values is Rotary. Their Vision, "Service Above Self" is underpinned by a set of standards and values defined in their 4 Way Test: "Of the things we think, say or do

1. Is it the TRUTH?

2. Is it FAIR to all concerned?
3. Will it build GOODWILL and BETTER FRIENDSHIPS?
4. Will it be BENEFICIAL to all concerned?"

I've never seen anyone in Rotary focus totally on just "the bottom line" and yet every year hundreds of millions of dollars are raised and re-distributed to individuals and communities in need.

Business and community leaders, many household names even in the international community, give generously of their time, money and commitment – all without seeking personal glory or publicity.

Every day, somewhere in the world, at barbecues and special functions people give dollars and support with no need to gain a tax deductable receipt.

Why? Because they see the *value* of the *values* of this service organisation. They choose to embrace those values.

Every leader in every walk of life has a choice to make; what are the values they will display in their leadership?

We can choose values that are positive; truthfulness, trust, respect, honesty, service-above-self, supportiveness, integrity, passion, benevolence and fairness.

Or we can choose just the opposite; untruthfulness, power, deceit, greed, self-interest, profit above people, or status.

Indeed, the only difference in leadership characteristics that set leaders such as Winston Churchill and Adolf Hitler or Mahatma Gandhi and the leaders of the extremist terrorist groups pervading our world today is Values.

They all have the ability to bring people together for a cause – good or bad. They all have the capacity of extolling their followers to even greater heights – good or bad. They all have the capacity to speak with a clear, articulate massage. To seek out those that can support them in their cause. To develop systems to bring their cause to life.

But it is their Values that set them apart. Good or bad. Positive or negative. Beneficial or destructive.

A perfect example of just how negative values can affect us all is the so-called Global Financial Crisis. The reason I say "so-called" is that, as I said in the Introduction, I believe what we suffered from was not a Financial Crisis but a Values Crisis.

You only need to look at the underpinning values that led the decision making of the major corporations that led us into this crisis – deceit, greed, lack of integrity and power – just to name a few.

The bottom line became the main driver. The return on investment, driven often by the shareholders demand for even greater, more sustainable returns on *their* investment fuelled the need to find ways to extract more from the market – which is made up of people and not just "market opportunities" – to satisfy this demand.

People seemed to ignore centuries of knowledge that shows that boom-times do not, and cannot, go on forever. That high growth, higher and higher returns come at a cost – to someone.

And when that cost is extracted, oh what a hue and cry we hear.

But here is the kicker. Even recently, despite all of the platitudes that corporations and financial institutions have learnt their lessons, we still see the same types of arrogant and deceitful actions being taken by some.

For instance, we still see banks manipulating the markets, and not disclosing to customers the full terms and conditions of their financial transactions.

But of course banks are easy targets. I should know. I was a State Manager for a bank; fortunately, a bank that was different and that valued its members – because the bank was owned by the members.

But what is the difference between them and the company that reduces the number of cookies or eggs in a pack or the size of the chocolate bar while maintaining the same overall sized packaging in order to give the _appearance_ that nothing has changed?

There is none really – merely the scale of things. It's all smoke and mirrors aimed at fooling – or deceiving – the customer!

Don't get me wrong. I am a businessman. I conduct workshops for major corporations and small businesses alike that are aimed at maximising profits.

Achieving the bottom-line profits for any business is important. Without profit there would be no real incentive for anyone to go into business – and that would be bad for jobs and our country.

But at what cost?

A Values Inspired Leader is one who looks at the values that guide their leadership decisions.

They incorporate those values into every aspect of their business and look for those values and build them in the people they employ.

They take the Vision of an organisation to heart, deliver a Mission based on results and underpin them both with Values that are based on integrity.

Curiously, applying such values does not come at a cost to the business. Rather it creates a loyalty that, long term, benefits all involved.

I should know. With them I helped build a billion-dollar business in under four years.

So, what does it take to be a Values Inspired Leader?

Well, that's what these 10 Lessons are all about.

- Lesson 1 -

There are two types of respect

– Lesson 1 –

There are two types of respect

I first learned about leadership at the very beginning of my time in the Royal Australian Air Force (RAAF). Indeed, that first lesson in leadership has since been reinforced many times over in both my professional and personal lives.

I learned that there are two types of respect given to leaders: the respect of their rank (or position) and the respect of the person.

Respect of rank is a given. Rank describes the position of an individual in the hierarchy of an organisation. You salute the rank even if you don't know or respect the individual.

Respect of the person is different. It is something that is earned, not just given for the sake of it. This respect takes time to develop and comes from really getting to know the person behind the rank. It is gained through the example set by that individual's actions and behaviour. This is the type of respect that may see others following that person to the death – no matter what rank they hold.

Respect of the person is much deeper than *any* respect of rank.

Case Study - The Pilot Officer.
I learned the difference between the two on my RAAF rookies' course. My flight would line up outside of our barracks every

morning in preparation for the daily inspection by our Drill Sergeant; and nearly every morning a young Pilot Officer would ride his pushbike past us on his way to the Flight Line.

Now, for those who don't know, a pilot officer is the most junior Air Force officer rank and usually applies to someone so fresh out of the Defence Force Academy that they still have pimples.

Our course orderly, Doug, had been in the armed services previously and right on cue he would bring the flight to attention, about turn and give his very best salute to this inexperienced officer. Then, to our great amusement the Pilot Officer would attempt to salute us in return while trying to maintain control of his bike—without fail!

What the Pilot Officer didn't recognise was that Doug, with the rest of the flight in full support, did this just to see his circus-like antics. He was so responsive to our display of respect for his rank that he was insistent on putting his own personal safety at risk. We were actually making use of his rank to mock him and, in so doing, we were showing absolutely no respect to him as an individual.

We only stopped when our sergeant, whom we did respect both in rank and as a person, threatened some form of grievous physical retribution on our whole flight for, "trying to kill by stupidity an individual who knows no better and is carried away with his new-found rank!"

Don't confuse respect of the rank or position as being respect for the person themselves.

A Word on real respect

Why is it that when new managers are promoted to a leadership role, so many of them beat their chest and demand that their staff respect *them* personally? But why *should* they be respected as individuals by their team? After all what have they done *personally* to *earn* their team's respect—other than getting promoted?

A Values Inspired Leader is someone who understands that real respect from the people they lead, respect that goes beyond that for their position and which is for the individual themselves, *is a respect that must be earned.*

The Values Inspired Leader knows it is *what* they do and *how* they do it that will earn them the real respect of the team.

They know they have to work to gain this respect and that it is not automatically given. They know it is what they *do* and not the work of others that generates this respect. They understand that reputation counts for little and that what they have done in the past is nowhere near as important as what they do now and in the future.

They know that true respect for them as an individual can only be given voluntarily and not forced from their team.

They know they must take on board all the lessons set out in this book in order to earn that respect.

Case Study - Julie: a leader to respect

One of the best leaders I have had the privilege to work with was Julie T. I met Julie while working with a major insurance company. It would be true to say that Julie was tough in some ways, but extremely fair. She expected much but also gave much. She encouraged her team and rewarded excellence. She showed her willingness to develop her staff and that she would stand and fight for them. On more than one occasion she "took-on" individuals in the national management team and stood up for what she knew was right.

However, Julie didn't display her great leadership skills only in the workplace. She also took them into the 'real' world and would stand up against poor management practices anywhere she found them.

One story that gained the team's respect (and which earned her "legend" status,) occurred when she was shopping at her local supermarket. She heard the Store Manager carrying on to one of his senior staff, in front of the customers and the other staff, about how some of his team were so pathetic. Apparently this was because one of his staff had dared to ask if they could have their scheduled morning tea break—even though it was busy and their break had already been delayed because of this.

As Julie progressed to the check-out, she (and everyone else,) continued to hear about this manager's problems with his poorly skilled staff and how hard they made his life. So, when she arrived at the check-out, she quietly asked the manager if she could have a word with him. She began by confirming that he did indeed have staff who performed poorly and who displayed behaviour that wasn't up to the standards he desired.

She then asked him if he had ever explained his expectations to his staff. When he stated that he hadn't and that he shouldn't have to anyway, Julie responded with a magnificent line, "Could I suggest that you don't have a staff problem? What you have is a management problem!"

As she left the store she was approached by staff members who thanked her for saying what she had—they had wanted to say such things for some time but felt they couldn't. She had not only earned her team's respect as a leader in the workplace, but she had also earned the respect of the staff at her supermarket. The more our team learned about Julie, the more highly we regarded her.

Values Inspired Leaders know that they have a position to fill and a role to perform. They understand that the traits and behaviour they display as a person, i.e., their own characteristics, personality and integrity, are what will lead their team to respect them.

Importantly though, they understand the difference between being liked and being respected. Values Inspired Leaders are willing to be disliked for what they do. For them respect is more important than being liked.

Far too often managers will attempt to do only the things that they think will be popular with their staff and hope to gain respect that way. Their teams certainly like the easy life that such a leader brings to the workplace but in the end this management style does not earn respect, it earns the exact opposite. Their team members will pick this up as a sign of weakness in their leader and *lose* respect for them as a result.

Values Inspired Leaders don't expect respect. They understand that it is an honour they must earn and that it can never be forced from their team. They are often humbled when they do receive it—but are pleased to have earned it.

That's what makes the Values Inspired Leader so special *and* so successful!

Questions for Values Inspired Leaders:

1. *Do I expect my team to respect me just because of the position I hold or because of what I do?*

2. *What have I done or what do I do to earn the respect of my team?*

3. *What do I need to do to earn the respect of my team?*

- Lesson 2 -

To earn respect, I must first give respect

– Lesson 2 –

To earn respect, I must first give respect

Have you ever noticed how a new manager will very often attempt to make their mark with a new team by changing everything?

It's what I call the "We'll do it _my_ way" syndrome.

Forget the fact that what has worked until now _has_ actually worked. The desire to change everything is more to do with the fact that what was working is the result of the previous leadership—so it must be removed.

It's almost like the Pharaohs of ancient Egypt removing all record of their predecessors in an attempt to have themselves recognised as the sole deity. Or, as I was once told, it's like the dog that has to leave their own very special mark on every lamp post. They have to do it simply to replace the scent left by any other dog.

It takes the strength of character of a Values Inspired Leader to recognise the good things that a previous leader has done. They recognise that they don't have to destroy everything that came before them in order to achieve great results into the future. They recognise that those things that have worked until now gives them a foundation to build on—no matter who was responsible for laying that foundation in the first place. They recognise it is not about point-scoring, but about building on what does work and going on from there to achieve even greater results.

I learned this lesson from the Bible, where it states, *"Don't make straight what God has made crooked"* (Ecc. 7:13). In other words, let the things that work ... work! After all, if it's good enough to work for God than who's to argue?

Yet so many new leaders try to change what works *simply in order to make their mark on the team*—to say "I have arrived. *I* am in charge!"

Consider how demoralising it must be for a team to have all their past efforts down-played and their way of doing things automatically discarded by a new "leader." Think how disrespectful it is for their team to be told, not in words but in actions, that absolutely everything they've been doing up to that point just isn't good enough anymore! Not one thing! Even a broken clock is correct twice a day.

Sure, there are teams, there are people, whose performance needs to be changed in order to achieve bigger and better things. And, there are those that will never fit in to any new way of achieving those required results and so will need to find new opportunities for their talents elsewhere. But to say that they are incapable of any good thing? But that is exactly what some new managers do. And it is a big mistake.

Remember Lesson 1—respect is earned?

How can any new leader expect to earn the respect *of* their team when their very first action is to show no respect *to* that team?

A Word on 'it works, so why change it?'

I recently spent three and a half years leading a magnificent team for a major bank. When I first moved into the role my team had three mobile mortgage lenders to service a city of only 330,000 people. When I left that number had increased to a total of ten sales staff.

Prior to me taking on the role, my new manager had been managing the team from an interstate office. When I started the job, he told me that I should seriously adjust the way in which one of my team was selling. My national manager didn't like his style.

When I left the job the national manager was still telling me the same thing. You see, I hadn't done anything in that time to change my lender's style. I considered that to do so would have been an act of lunacy on my part.

Why? Well, when I joined the team Andrew was the number one sales person in Australia. In fact, he would remain in that position for the next three years, when another team member would claim that mantle.

Let me put Andrew's efforts into perspective. He was one of a national sales team of about 80 and he was operating in one of the smallest markets in the country. Compare our 330,000 population with that of other major capital cities that weighed in with over 4,000,000 people each.

Now, for a lender in the mortgage industry to be recognised as pretty good they would probably average about $45m to $50m a year in sales, back then. Andrew achieved sales in excess of $109m in a single year he alone sold more than double the industry average. His average annual sales for the three and a half years were well over $80m.

So what was it that my boss didn't like about Andrew's style? It turned out to be the length of time Andrew took in the face-to-face sales interview with the client. A lender usually takes an hour to an hour and a half for an interview but Andrew often only took 30 minutes.

However, instead of jumping in and immediately changing things, I sat back and watched how he managed his sales process. I discovered that Andrew actually conducted much of his interview by questioning clients over the phone while travelling between appointments (hands free!).

This meant that when he saw the customer face-to-face, he already knew exactly what the customer wanted and usually only needed to tidy up any last minute details and complete the paperwork. What for most sales people is dead time was for Andrew productive time.

Now, was that the style I would have used? No, but I'm not that organised! I would have preferred the same style as my boss; the one where you sit in front of the customer, ask all the questions and complete the selling interview in one appointment. But

Andrew's style worked. It's what had made him number one. I would have been a fool to force him to change.

Ironically, Andrew was eventually pipped to the post by a teammate and the former national number two lender—Rhonda—and she used the sales style that both my boss and I preferred. Which only goes to prove that *both* styles worked.

A Word on 'the right time to make a change'

Sometimes the best thing a new leader can do is to step back, bite their tongue and do nothing—except watch and learn.

Only after that do you know what is really happening in the team; *after you have gathered the facts for yourself*, assessed the strengths and weaknesses of each individual, and worked out how those strengths and weaknesses add to or detract from the team's results *should any leader dare to make a change.* Don't rely on second opinions.

"My way or the highway" is not necessarily the only way that a task or outcome can be achieved. Often there are several ways to succeed and achieve a fantastic result. If the process being followed is legal, not detrimental to the needs of the business, or destructive in any way, does it really matter than *exactly* how that result is achieved? What is more important—the result or the process?

I do not know everything. I wish I knew more. However, what I have learned through my experience and my training—both in the classroom and on-the-job, is that through it all, I have gained the ability to perform the roles in which I find myself. These roles are merely a reflection of those abilities gained over time.

This is true for everyone. Each of us has skills, attributes, talents, mannerisms and characteristics that make us good at what we do. The role anyone is given is a reward for how well they have learned to use their level of knowledge and their abilities.

Nevertheless, the experiences and talents of one person are not those of another. The characteristics, attributes, skills and mannerisms of one person are bound to be different from anyone else—even between those performing the same roles. With this in mind, why then would a Values Inspired Leader expect their team members to all be the same and perform identically to one another? They don't!

The Values Inspired Leader acknowledges the differences.

The Values Inspired Leader embraces and encourages those differences.

The Values Inspired Leader acknowledges that there is more than one way to achieve an outstanding result.

The Values Inspired Leader uses the combined skills of the team and their results to date in order to go on to even greater achievements.

The Values Inspired Leader acknowledges that respect is a two-way street.

Values Inspired Leaders know that before any team can show real respect to a leader, and not just to the position they hold, then that leader must first show respect to the individual team members.

They must show respect to what those individuals have achieved. They must show respect for their skills and their knowledge. They must show respect to them as human beings.

They must show respect in such a way that it says, "I trust you."

Questions for Values Inspired Leaders:

4   What is it about each of my individual team members that I respect?

5   How do I show my respect to the team?

– Lesson 3 –

I have to trust my people

- Lesson 3 -

I have to trust my people

When most people start a new job they get the standard induction speech about their role, what is expected of them and so on. However, when I give my new staff the usual "Welcome to your new job" speech, I first let them know what I think of them.

It's a simple message—"You're here because I believe you can do the job, otherwise I wouldn't have hired you. I *trust* you to make this role successful."

In all the companies which I have helped to develop across different countries, I have discovered one undeniable truth. In the vast majority of cases, the people employed by those companies knew what they had to do in their roles to make those roles successful.

They knew that if everyone worked at making their part of the business a success then the entire company would be successful.

A Word on 'trusting the team: they know what they need to do to be successful.'

A few years ago I was asked to work with an overseas company in order to raise the service delivery levels of their teams. I had worked with the same company in Australia but the last thing the staff in the overseas offices needed was for some Smart Alec "expert" to tell them "This is how we did it in Australia".

So, instead of *telling* them, I *asked* them how they could make the service they delivered a "Wow" experience for their customers.

Then, over several weeks and many workshops, the staff developed the service delivery standards that were to change the way they were perceived in the market. By following these standards, they then managed to raise their customer contact centre from being unrated in national surveys, to being the number two rated company in the country.

Ironically, those service standards were almost identical to the ones introduced by the parent company in Australia. However, the overseas team hadn't been told what those standards were. They had come up with their own benchmarks all by themselves.

Simply asking the people who actually did the job for their ideas on improving the way the company did business resulted in major changes to customer service delivery standards and great business success. Because the staff now owned that process.

It was a matter of *trusting* the staff to have the answers. After all, they wanted to be successful personally and took pride in working in their jobs for the company. These staff members were just like many of people the Values Inspired Leader will encounter.

Case Study - The ultimate in trust: Ricardo Semler

Ricardo Semler must be the ultimate example of a Values Inspired Leader who trusted his people.

At the time Semler took over his father's Brazilian shipbuilding supplies business, SEMCO S.A., in 1980, it had started to struggle and looked like it was in real trouble. What Semler did then was absolutely revolutionary in the field of management. He handed over the running of the company to his people. Totally and completely. He *trusted* them to do what was needed in order to turn the company around.

Not only did the company become extremely profitable and successful but Semler's leadership techniques became a case study for blue chip companies such as IBM*. SEMCO grew from a $US4m company with 90 employees in 1982, into a $US212m company with over 3,000 employees in 2003 with a growth rate of up to 40% per annum, making it one of Brazil's leading businesses.

Semler was so successful in his leadership style that one day he arrived at work to find he no longer had an office! His team had decided he didn't need one and they needed the space for some more important function in the process of making the business more successful.

How many managers would trust their people enough to hand over complete control of their area of operations to those very same people?

Not that you *have* to do so in order to be a Values Inspired Leader but isn't that what trust should be about? That the people you

---

* You can read his story in the book "Maverick" by Ricardo Semler, published by Random House Business Books.

place in your team have what it takes to make success an everyday word?

So why is it that so many managers feel it necessary to micro-manage the people they have employed and then try to do the job those very people were hired to do?

It's like the manager I knew who employed highly experienced staff and then had each of them pass their work to himself for final approval. Instead of trusting his team to do the right thing (and possibly allowing them to make a mistake), this manager created a situation where some of the team wouldn't make a decision unless he approved it first.

Not only were the team hamstrung in decision-making but the manager then found himself under great pressure as work began to backlog to an almost intolerable level. Only when he changed; let go and trusted in his team's abilities did his workload diminish. That team soon became the number one team nationally, setting productivity records in the process.

Trust!

A Values Inspired Leader trusts their people while a manager manages their staff.

If you can't trust the people in your team to do the job they were employed to do, then you shouldn't have hired them in the first place!

Questions for
Values Inspired Leaders

6   How do I show that I trust my team members?

– Lesson 4 –

I will be promoted to my own level of incompetence,
so I should employ people who make me look good!

– Lesson 4 –

I will be promoted to my own level of incompetence, so I should employ people who make me look good!

In the Air Force we had a saying, "You will be promoted to your level of incompetence." Another way to look at it is that the higher you go in an organisation the greater the likelihood that you don't know what you are doing!

Of course, all that is said with tongue firmly in cheek; although it does contain a grain of truth. We can all probably recall a manager we have worked with who couldn't have done our job in a pink fit.

Well I have been one of those leaders, and guess what? I discovered I *wasn't* employed as a leader because I could do the jobs of my staff as well as they could do them. I was hired because I was capable of finding the right people to do the jobs that needed doing; I was capable of looking after the strategic aspects of achieving our individual and team targets, and I was able to support and lead the team while they did their jobs.

In other words, for me to be successful as a leader, I had to find people who were far more qualified than me at those roles and get them to work for me.

Someone who is brilliant at their job is not necessarily going to perform well as a leader, and vice-versa. How often have you seen someone who is technically great at their job go on to fail in a leadership role?

Does that mean that leaders don't have to understand their industry or what their people do? No!

To be truly effective as a leader they must have a high level of understanding for their industry and they must understand the roles of their people. A leader also needs to be able to see and understand the issues and challenges that each of their team face as they perform their roles day-to-day.

However, that doesn't mean they have to show themselves to be as good as, or better than, their own people in order to lead them.

A Values Inspired Leader just has to show their team that their leader understands what it is that they face when they go out to conquer the world for the business; and that their leader trusts them to do just that.

This book is dedicated to an absolutely brilliant sales team; one I had the privilege to lead. In every aspect of their roles they achieved the highest level of sales and service. They set the standard for every other team in that company. One of the best compliments to their abilities was given to me by the person who took over my responsibility for this wonderful team. He believed that this was the best team he had seen in over 20 years in the industry.

I have often been asked how we achieved the results we did as a team; how I became a Values Inspired Leader. The answer is simple. I employed people who could do their jobs better than I could do them.

Prior to taking on the task of establishing a new team, in a relatively untapped market, I had had only 18 months' experience with the company—and that was as their National Training & Development Manager. My experience in the actual operational side of the business was limited, to say the least! I had written product training manuals and had worked in a related industry for many years, but I had never had the day-to-day experiences that my team had. In some ways I was a novice.

Each member I employed in my team had 15 to 20 years' experience in their field. They were good at what they did. In fact, they were better than good. They were brilliant.

It was nothing for all the team members to be ranked in the top 10 of the national salesforce, and that was with most holding all but one of the top 5 positions. They were supported by an equally experienced support team who constantly set new national records themselves.

By hiring people who were better than me at the jobs they were employed to do I was, unashamedly, made to look good—and we achieved great results and outstanding business growth.

A Values Inspired Leader understands and accepts this principle of taking on board the best people possible—even if those people are far better than the leader is at doing the job *the team members* are employed to do.

Values Inspired Leaders are not scared by the success of their team—they rejoice in it. Values Inspired Leaders are not afraid to share the success of the team where the success should be shared—with the team. A Values Inspired Leader is one who is secure in the knowledge that their own role in the success of the team is that of being the team leader, not the team 'doer.'

A Values Inspired Leader is secure in their own position and is not undermined by the success of the team or any individual member of it.

On the other hand, a manager who does not understand or accept these principles will often be scared of doing this. After all, how can you control people who are better than you? How can you show them how to do their job when they can do it better than you can? For many there is the inherent fear that they will not be promoted—not get to climb the corporate ladder—if they aren't seen as being better than the people they have working for them. They want to present a picture which says that their people are inferior and it is their own, the manager's own, superiority that makes it all work.

Invariably, a manager like this will employ a weak team and not even realise it; simply because they will feel comfortable with being in charge. In effect what they are doing is limiting the team's success to their own leader's level of incompetence.

What managers like this fail to see is that it is only through employing the very best team possible that they can avoid being promoted only to their own level of incompetence. This holds true even if that means hiring people with better knowledge or skills in those team roles, or by developing their people and enabling them to be the very best that *they* can be.

I learned years ago that Values Inspired Leaders know that they must become *dispensable* in their role in order to move onwards and upwards. In other words, they need to have people capable of taking over from them in order to be promoted themselves.

Some managers work so hard at creating an empire around themselves, at becoming indispensable, that they fail to see that this empire then becomes a factor which limits their future leadership aspirations. They fail to develop—both themselves and the members of their team. Then, by default, they find that they have indeed been promoted to their level of (in)competence and that this is where they will stay. They have succeeded at being seen as OK at their job, but not as a future star.

This lack of a structure for ensuring staff development is one of the major issues I have encountered when coaching companies— they simply don't have any succession plans! They don't think of developing their people to take on future roles, or of the value there is in having someone ready to step into an opening within the company should one become available.

A Word on 'succession planning.'

Whether it be through fear, insecurity, incompetence, negligence or a simple lack of understanding, very few managers spend the time necessary to develop their people. Very few companies have an active succession plan in place; one that allows anyone from any level of the company to develop the skills and attributes necessary to rise to the next level in the company and their career.

Yes, many companies champion on-going career development; they even measure this as a key element in any 360-degree staff feedback questionnaire. However, when it comes to investing time, money and effort into that development there seems to be a shortfall of real commitment.

The long term investment benefits that come from a company having a clearly defined career development programme are huge, even though the initial cost of developing people may be high. When you develop people from within your organisation, you then instil the culture and vision of that organisation into every aspect and level of its operations as those prospective leaders take on more challenging roles within your business.

Many an organisation has failed in its long term objectives by not having developed their own people and then finding they need to employ someone external to the company. Then, too late they realise that this new external influence doesn't fit the culture of the organisation, or that the new recruit acts in a way that contradicts the vision and mission of the company.

One organisation I worked with replaced their Executive Marketing Manager more often than some people change their underwear. It was a young, growing organisation and had, in most cases, promoted people into the role—people who had what appeared to be the right marketing or sales qualifications.

While these people knew their business and understood the company intimately; having grown with it from the early years, they were usually placed into the role with little—if any—training, mentoring or executive coaching. When I worked with them, I often felt, sadly, that these good people were being put into a 'sink or swim' position.

The company's one experience of employing someone from outside had ended quicker than an ice-cream on a summer's day—and with a fair few burnt relationships on the way. That person simply hadn't understood the special relationship this company had with their sector of the market; a relationship that made this company so different.

Companies let themselves down by not developing great people just on the off-chance that those great people may be the ones who will step up into a leadership role once it becomes vacant, or if a new role is created. They fail by not providing a continuous leadership or executive development programs that takes an already talented person and develops their skills even further.

They also let themselves down by promoting talented individuals into leadership roles and then not providing them with a mentor or coach; in order to guide them in that role. (What? Are they supposed to be great leaders automatically just because they've been promoted?)

Values Inspired Leadership, at an individual level and as a corporate citizen within the broader community, starts with employing great people and then developing them even further. Companies like McDonalds grow dramatically because of one major difference—they develop their leadership from within. They concentrate on always making their people better at what they do.

Values Inspired Leadership means never being afraid to employ people better than you. Values Inspired Leaders recognise their own limitations and are willing to plug the gaps caused by those limitations with other people who are great at what they do.

Values Inspired Leadership means never being afraid of developing people to the point where they can be promoted—even if that means that they could be promoted over the head of their own Values Inspired Leader!

Values Inspired Leadership means not being fearful that the person being developed may end up being better than the person they answer to. In fact, a Values Inspired Leader will rejoice when someone they have helped develop is the one being promoted. They will celebrate the success of their people.

That's just one more thing that makes a Values Inspired Leader so special.

Questions for Values Inspired Leaders

7   *What am I good at?*

8   *What are my team members good at?*

9   *Does my team have all the skills and abilities I need it to have in order to achieve my business goals?*

10   *What additional skills and abilities do I need in order to achieve my business goals?*

11   *How am I developing my people?*

12   *Who am I developing to take over from me?*

13   *How do I need to develop them in order to better prepare them to take over from me?*

- Lesson 5 -

I work to make it work

– Lesson 5 –

I work to make it work

Having the right people in your team is one thing but it takes more than just having the right people to ensure success. Values Inspired Leaders understand that success over the long term is built on flexibility and the desire to always strive to be better. They understand that outstanding success comes from everyone in an organisation constantly working at getting it right – and then some.

A Word on being flexible

A Values Inspired Leader is flexible. No, I'm not talking about the being able to bend-over-and-touch-your-toes type flexible – a position often considered important for managers to learn for some reason! Although, fitness is important to a Values Inspired Leader's ability to cope with the stresses of their role.

No, I'm talking about the flexibility to change tack at a moment's notice in order to be able to take advantage of an opportunity. It's the flexibility to define what works and what doesn't and to get rid of what doesn't —even if it dents one's pride.

It is the flexibility to change day-to-day operations in order to meet the requirements of the day. It's being flexible enough to place more emphasis on the important strategies that will drive success rather than the mundane, less important but still required-at-some-stage tactics that take away from that immediate success.

For instance: meetings! Some managers insist that meetings must take place at a certain time every week. Yes, meetings can be important. And yes, you can convey important messages or gather important information at meetings. And yes, it is important for the team to get together on a regular basis. But how many of us know of meetings that have been an absolute waste of time? How many managers use meetings more as a control mechanism rather than as a dialogue session?

So why, when times are tough and the team is expected to work harder at achieving their targets, would anyone but an incompetent manager call a meeting that wasn't really required? Yet that is exactly what some managers insist on! "It's Monday, therefore we have to have a meeting because we always have a meeting on Monday!"

Makes sense to a manager!

A Values Inspired Leader knows that there are other ways to keep in touch with and convey messages to their team if necessary. A Values Inspired Leader is flexible enough to gather the information they require without calling a meeting. A Values Inspired Leader only calls meetings when meetings are really needed.

But that's just meetings. A Values Inspired Leader is flexible in all other areas when needed, but is not so flexible as to just give into the team because the team want change. They are flexible for a success principle—one that ensures that the right people are doing the right thing, the right way.

A Word on 'right people, right process, right number.'

A Values Inspired Leader recognises that success comes from aiming high and that having stretch targets is nothing to be feared. Yet many managers work hard to set the lowest possible measure of success that they can for their team—a target they *know* the team *can* achieve—just so they can say they made their targets. They actually aim for mediocrity!

A Values Inspired Leader understands that in order to achieve outstanding, stretch targets they require:

> The right people;

>> doing the right "thing";

>>> the right way; and,

>>>> the right number of times.

An example of this process in action (or not, as the case may be) can be seen when observing the staff manning displays at trade shows or such similar events.

Now, the one aim of the companies which set up stands at these shows is to create enough customer interest in order to generate a considerable number of leads, appointments and/or sales. Yet far too often the people manning these stands seem to operate at odds to this aim.

Companies will normally outfit these stands with qualified sales staff; people who know their stuff when it comes to selling the products or services on offer. In this way they meet the first criterion of having *the right people*.

The role of the salesperson is to entice the passer-by into seeking more information or to book a sales appointment. However, some stand operators just let the customer wander into the stand, with no call to action—which just encourages window shopping and not action taking.

However, really proactive stand operators will have something to draw people into the stand. In this example, let's suppose that the way to attract future customers is this: when passers-by enter the stand, they are then given a pen and a card with some questions for them to answer about the materials displayed. When they get to the other end of the stand, they will then hand the filled-out card to a salesperson who gives the customer a free gift. So the second criterion is met. The salespeople *are doing the right "thing"* and the right process for success is put in place.

But what if the staff gets the potential customer into the stand and then fails to take the steps necessary to set the appointment or give further information? In this case the lack of success can be attributed to the right people doing the right thing—getting people into the stand and answering the questions—but in one step of the process they're not doing it in the right way. It only takes skipping one step of a known success process for it to fail.

Just look at the fast food chain, McDonalds. They have perfected the art of following a seamless sameness to success. They have a process which must be followed by every operator in every store everywhere in the world, for the same product. A cheeseburger in America has the sameness of a cheeseburger in Australia or Britain or New Zealand or Russia. McDonalds teach their people to do the exact same steps time and time again. Consistency is the one ensured outcome from this. And that consistency is why McDonalds makes the profits it does.

This consistency in product and service delivery has led to economists using the price of a Big Mac as a measure of the state of the economy of individual countries worldwide. Officially it is called The Big Mac Index. I wonder if Ray Croc ever envisaged that his hamburgers could determine the next great economic policy of a nation; and to think we *joke* about government being full of clowns!

So, for this example of getting appointments at the trade show stand the team members must do the right thing the right way according to the third criterion.

But what if the staff are doing the right thing the right way—getting the appointments—but just aren't getting enough people into the stand? Think about how often you have seen people manning these stands looking bored, paying no attention to the passers-by, and doing nothing to encourage people to move beyond their reluctance and into the stand.

We can pretty much assume that the results for the stand holder wouldn't be as good as they should. In this case the right people would be doing the right thing the right way, but just not often enough to get the required result.

And so it is for any business that wants to succeed. If the market is tight, or the situation you face is difficult, then you may have to work harder than you would in an easier market or situation to achieve the required result. The team may need to work harder at generating more leads, or at contacting more people, or both, to make enough appointments to meet targets. In any business, if you don't see enough people than you won't get enough business to get the results you want.

In this way, each stage of the process is just as important as the other stages if you are to succeed.

Values Inspired Leaders understand the importance of this whole process. They also understand the importance of never accepting that the process that works now is the one that will work in the future. They are always looking for ways to improve—to be better.

A Word on 'the Continuous Improvement Process.'
The Continuous Improvement Process (CIP) is a necessary evil for team and business success. Without it you could never grow, improve, or change to meet market demands.

Without a CIP, the leader must accept that at some stage their team or their business will start to go backwards in comparison with market trends and with other companies who do use a CIP. It is folly to simply accept that what is done now will always be the best that can be done.

Once your opposition work out what you are doing to generate dynamic business and market growth you can be assured that they will seek a way to regain their market share from yours— either through better products, services or gimmicks.

A dynamic company is one that always seeks to stay ahead of their opposition. The companies that use a CIP to maximum effect are those that are always evaluating their performance and that of every member of their teams.

"Everyone" includes the Values Inspired Leader and any other member of the executive and Board.

No matter how good they *think* they are, no leader is above improvement. For instance, I *think* I can play a perfect round of golf, but those who have seen me play—and I use that term very, very loosely in this instance—know the truth of the matter. Well, some managers out there think that they are playing a 63 round when they are effectively shooting 112.

Values Inspired Leaders are open to feedback on their own performance; from those above them and their team members. They will evaluate the validity of that feedback and take action to improve where appropriate.

The loneliness of leadership demands that leaders display certain characteristics or take positions at odds to popular perceptions— *if these positions are the right stance to take.*

This means they don't implement all of the changes their team wants them to make. What a Values Inspired Leader tries to do is attempt to find a way by which their own performance can be improved. This may be through simply displaying one of their characteristics better, or reviewing how a decision or position they have taken could have been better communicated to the team.

The more a Leader is open to feedback, the more their team is open to a CIP themselves. Feedback within the team environment must be handled properly.

A simple, yet valuable method I have learned for managing this is: PIP/RIP.

    Praise   **I**n   **P**ublic

    Reproach   **I**n   **P**rivate

Share the successes of your people in the open—but let any reproach, any recommendation for improvement, be done in private. It's all part of showing respect to your people.

One mistake companies make in applying a CIP is to use it as a tool of punishment, instead of as a development opportunity. Same tool. Two totally different approaches.

Used as a punishment, it destroys trust and openness instead of building it. However, use it as a development opportunity, with all the right support for the improvement to take place, and a CIP will make your people and your business better and stronger.

Having said that, let me point out that without the support of everyone in the company and a commitment to really make change happen, CIP will become merely a tool of disappointment.

Some companies mouth the words of CIP. They put feedback strategies into place and dutifully vocalise their commitment to the change program they have established. Then, in the cold, hard light of day, that commitment gives way to the perceived realities of both a commercial world and the perceived "cost" of implementing change.

That's why the results of 360-degree staff feedback surveys often flag the same issues for development opportunities year-in and year-out. And managers wonder why? They wonder why their staff feel that the surveys are a joke; why their staff think they are just management's way of paying lip-service to the issues of concern their team feel are important to them!

If more managers looked at the cost of change as an investment in growth and a means of retaining staff, which actually results in lower cost with a high return on investment, they could become Values Inspired Leaders!

While Values Inspired Leaders may not be able to change a company's development policy, they *can* take steps to implement what changes they can in their team environment. These leaders also take steps to seek out their own means of personal development—they don't hang around waiting for someone to do it for them.

A Continuous Improvement Process is a valuable tool for ensuring that everything that can be done is in place for success. It enables a Leader to evaluate what works and what doesn't, and enables a team to provide any ideas they may have for improvements.

But be warned. Having this level of open, frank and trusting discussions can often raise issues that will put a Leader in a position where they will have to fight for change or take a stand on an issue. This is where a Values Inspired Leader really earns their stripes.

A Word on 'openness and trust.'

As a leader you will be dealing with people; and people come with emotions, issues, problems and, hopefully, solutions. The old adage "There is the door, leave your personal problems outside" is no more valid than putting people in jail simply because they disagree with someone.

Yet that is exactly how some people are expected to operate at work.

Values Inspired Leaders recognise that what happens on the home front, can and does affect what happens in the workplace. Equally, they acknowledge that what happens at work or in the team can also be reflected on the home front.

Values Inspired Leaders work at creating an environment where team members feel they can discuss any issue whatsoever, be it work related or personal, without fear of reprisal, reproach or derision. The Leader becomes a confidant virtually by default. They become a coach, a mentor or just an ear to bend—but not necessarily a friend.

Their team members must feel secure that whatever is said in this context will remain confidential and that, where action is required, it will be taken in the most appropriate and supportive manner.

The team must know that, no matter what happens, their dignity and trust will be maintained. It is a trust that once breached is almost impossible to rebuild. It is something that a Values Inspired Leader treats with total respect.

This trust translates directly into the Continuous Improvement Process; where continuous improvement ensures that the Values Inspired Leader has the best people doing the best job in ways that achieve the best results. They are always striving to get it right and doing it better for the team.

Questions for Values Inspired Leaders

14   How am I flexible?

15   Does my team trust me, and can they talk openly with me?

16   Do I hold grudges or seek to get even with people when I am criticised or told the truth?

17   What is my Continuous Improvement Process?

18   Do I ensure I Praise in Public and Reproach in Private (PIP RIP)?

– Lesson 6 –

I am there to serve my team, not to be its servant

– Lesson 6 –

I am there to serve my team, not to be its servant

This is probably the hardest lesson to put into practice.

It is hard to apply because it contradicts the popular delusion regarding the near-divinity of managers. You know the old canard: *"Rule 1: The manager is always right.*
Rule 2: In case the manager is wrong, refer to Rule 1."

As a result, many managers think and act in a way that is contrary to what leadership is all about. In my experience, many managers make the mistake of believing that the team is there to support them in the pursuit of the manager's own goals. While that may be true to some extent, to believe it as an absolute would be wrong.

Yes, the team does support the leader in pursuit of their targets; but for that to happen effectively a leader must first *support their team,* totally and unreservedly.

This total support comes through ensuring that: -

1. Everything is in place for the team to be successful and achieve outstanding results; and

2. Team members have someone they can talk to and feel free to openly discuss issues with—without the risk of recrimination; and

3. The team have a champion who will fight the battles that need to be fought on their behalf.

In effect, leaders place themselves in a position to serve the team.

1. Ensuring everything is in place for success.

No team can achieve outstanding results if they don't have the right support available to achieve those results. The Values Inspired Leader's role is to create an environment that generates success. This covers all aspects of the team's operations and includes, but isn't limited to, such things as:

- Having a consistent vision across all levels of the business;
- Having a clear and consistent leadership approach across, and at every level of, the whole organisation;
- Having the correct processes in place;
- Using the right marketing approach for each individual market;
- Having the right promotional material on hand;
- Identifying and developing opportunities for growth;
- Having the right reporting processes in place;
- Initialising a reward and recognition programme;
- Having an appropriate feedback mechanism;

- Building the right relationships both internally and externally;
- Having the right level of staff in the right places;
- Having a Plan B and C and Z; and
- Only having meetings when required and not just for the sake of it.

As a Values Inspired Leader you will define exactly what each of these mean for *your* team in *your* market. Values Inspired Leaders are always ready to be flexible in their approach and ready to move quickly in order to achieve success. They recognise that what works in one market or situation may not be what works in another – even with the same product or service being offered in each.

My brilliant team successfully took our products to a wide range of market demographics and achieved a dramatic growth in our market share. However, for the team to achieve the results it did, we needed to employ different sales strategies for each market segment. For example, one major market sector consisted of "white collar" government employees who were office-bound and had a high level of computer skills, while another major market was in the construction industry where there wasn't a computer in sight.

When we were courting the office-bound customers we used: emails; the internet; seminars, and muffin/cookie days, amongst other things. We also dressed in slightly more formal attire.

On the other hand, when we were wooing the construction industry we used site barbecues and short, sharp information sessions held during smoko breaks and lunch-room sit-downs and we dressed appropriately for the environment—right down to the safety boots and hard hats!

Same city, different markets, different strategies, different support requirements.

As the team's leader my role was simple. I had to ensure that we:

- approached each market segment in such a way as to maximise our outcomes;
- had the right relationships in place in order to get us onto sites and in front of potential customers;
- had the right marketing material available and the right equipment available to use;
- gave appropriate presentations, and that
- we had the right people giving those presentations.

Even seemingly insignificant issues had to be looked at in order for us to succeed. This included simple things like where we parked the company cars at any event the team attended. The locations were chosen in order to achieve maximum brand awareness among our prospective clients.

The question is, as a leader what do *you* need to do to ensure your team has everything in place they require to achieve the success you envisage for them?

2. Ensuring the team have someone to talk to

For some managers, the statement, "My door is always open", is just a platitude. Yes, the door may be open but does the manager really want to hear from their staff? Or are they the kind of manager who says, "Tell me honestly…" and then woe betide any person who does!

A Values Inspired Leader is someone whose team members feel that they can talk to, and with whom they feel free to openly discuss issues, without risking recrimination. This applies no matter what the issue—even if the subject matter is the leader them self.

Ego inspired dialogue is not of interest to a Values Inspired Leader. Instead, they are genuinely interested in hearing both their team's issues and suggested solutions.

And that is the crunch word—*solutions*! A Values Inspired Leader encourages the airing of issues that come complete with solutions. Not that they have to be the 'right' solutions, or the 'only' solution or the solution that 'has' to be used.

The point is more that the Values Inspired Leader encourages team input, and creates an environment where their staff can be a team of thinkers and action people and not just a team of complainers. It's all about approaching a problem with the attitude of "how can we," instead of "it's their (name anyone else) fault".

Achievers not blamers. Values Inspired People not whining

wimps!

This open dialogue is all part of building trust.

3. Ensuring the team have a champion

A Values Inspired Leader recognises that at times there are things that they need to stand up and fight for on behalf of their team. This doesn't mean they have to *win* the fights—but they do need to fight them.

They also understand that they don't have to take on every issue, just those that need a champion. They realise that their team needs to know that their leader is willing to stand up for them if required.

Often those in a leadership role will steer clear of taking on an issue with those above them, most probably due to a fear of being seen as someone who rocks the boat. A Values Inspired Leader recognises that if something is important enough to rock the boat for, then that is what they have to do.

They also recognise that it is no good just sounding off and making a noise about it. A Values Inspired Leader will collect all the data they need to support their case and then provide a logical argument for the change they propose. They know they will need answers to the questions they will be asked. After all, they expect their team to present the solutions with the problems, so it is the least that can be expected of them personally!

They will also look for those who can help champion their cause.

However, a Values Inspired Leader knows when to draw a line in the sand and acknowledge that some issues, no matter how cogent the arguments, will not lead to remedial action by those above them.

When that happens, they will continue to demonstrate and encourage maximum performance for success. A team that knows their Leader has gone in to fight for them will accept that some battles can't be won. They will be disappointed—but at least they will know that their Leader stood up for them.

On the other hand, and importantly, a Values Inspired Leader also knows that there will be times when they will need to have the courage to disagree with their team and take a position contrary to that which is popular.

Martin Luther King Jnr. said that, *"The ultimate measure of a man is not where he stands in moments of comfort, but where he stands at times of challenge and controversy".*

A Word on 'not being a servant of the team.'

Making and delivering hard decisions is part and parcel of being a Values Inspired Leader. It comes with the job. A leader knows that their decisions may not be popular with their team. They are fully aware that they are not participating in a popularity contest but acting in a leadership role.

A team must know that a Values Inspired Leader will fight for them—yet they must also know that their Leader won't just roll over and do what they want simply because their team wants it.

They must know that their Leader will serve them, but not be subservient to them.

This means that a Values Inspired Leader must learn how to deliver difficult news. They must seek out the positive points and use those to sell whatever decision has been made. They have to understand that at times they will be required to protect those who are their seniors in the organisation.

Often a leader will find themselves in a position where they can't divulge every reason behind why a decision was made. This is something that the team need to know. They need to know that their Leader understands their position and their arguments; and accept that this is the action that must be taken anyway.

How a Leader delivers that message will determine how well that decision is accepted.

There is nothing more disrespectful than telling team members (as have some managers I know) that, "That's the way it is and if you don't like it, there's the door." Adults can bear bad news as long as they are treated as adults and not as ignorant nuisances.

American President Calvin Coolidge stated that, *"No man was ever honoured for what he has received. Honour has been the reward for what he gave."*

Respect and honour, two of the key elements in recognising a Values Inspired Leader, are earned not by what the team does for the leader but for what the leader does for the team.

The example set by the Leader in both standing up *for* their team and in standing up *to* their team is what makes for a Values Inspired Leader. The actions of a Leader speak louder than any words they could ever utter. As they say in the classics, 'talk is cheap'. Actions are the currency on which a Leader's greatness is built.

A true Leader displays "True Leadership" by the way they act.

Questions for
Values Inspired Leaders

19 How do I support my team fully and ensure that everything is in place for them to achieve what I want them to achieve?

20 What do I need to do to improve the way I support my team?

21 How do I show I am willing to stand up for my team?

22 How do I prepare my arguments?

23 How do I deliver difficult news and do I sell the positives?

24 How do I stop myself from being subservient to my team?

- Lesson 7 -

A true leader is one whose boots are the first to hit the ground and are the last ones to leave!

– Lesson 7 –

A true leader is one whose boots are the first to hit the ground and are the last ones to leave!

Some people show their leadership skills by staying in the background while letting their team do all the dirty work. Hitler was an example of that style.

Others stay hidden away only long enough for their team to do all the hard work before emerging to claim the victory as their own. We can all probably think of a boss or manager like that.

A Values Inspired Leader is one who understands the value of *this* lesson—that a true leader leads from the front and shares in the duty to be done.

US Army Lieutenant-General Harold Moore is not a name with which most people would be familiar. During the Vietnam War, "Hal" Moore was the Battalion Commander of the US 1st Battalion, 7th Cavalry. On 14 November, 1965 he led his troops into what is regarded as the first major battle of that war; one which took place between the Americans and North Vietnamese. Over several days his 450 troops battled against over 2,000 North Vietnamese regulars in the La Drang Valley.

As a leader he is one person who lived this Values Inspired Leadership lesson. He lived by the adage that his boots would be the first to touch enemy territory and the last to leave it.

Where his troops went, he went; leading from the front. What his troops experienced, he experienced too; and when his troops were tired, weary and suffering, he was there with them—being a Leader. Then when the battle was over, when the last of his troops, living or dead, were lifted from the battlefield, only then did he leave.

Fortunately, most of us will never be called upon to lead troops into a live-fire war zone. But every leader will be called upon to do the job they are paid to do—and that is to lead.

If a leader were meant to sit in the background and push their people, then they wouldn't be called Leaders; they would be called Pushers. And that doesn't sound too good does it?

Maybe you can remember working for a boss who expected you to be at work early or work back late, even though they came in late or left early themselves. Maybe you have been one of those people who have been asked to work late or longer hours in order to complete some task, only for your manager to arrive at the moment of glory, ready to take all the personal recognition for a job well done. Or maybe you have worked over a weekend without a leader in sight. Well, you are not that far removed from the experience many team members have of how supposed leaders behave.

Once, when in a major leadership role, I attended a weekend function being held by another interstate office in order to see what I could learn about running a similar event for my own team. Surprisingly, I found that not one of the managers from the interstate office were programmed to be at the function, not once over the whole weekend. Obviously it was good enough for their team members to give up their weekend and attend the function, but it wasn't good enough for any of the management team to give up theirs.

How did their team feel about that? Probably the same way any team feels when their manager leads from behind or are absent-from-duty—disappointed, let down, angry, bitter, belittled, not wanting to be where they were and disrespectful. They had no respect for no-show leaders.

When it came time for my own state to run their function, I made certain that I was there in the days leading up to the event, putting in with the team whatever was needed to be done to ensure it all went off successfully. I was there throughout the weekend, giving up my time just as my team were giving up theirs.

One thing I have learned is that teams may not want to do the job they are asked to do, but they will put in the effort and do it if their leader is there with them. They will feel they are part of a complete effort to succeed when the leader is willing to be there first and leave last. It's not that the leader *has* to be there all the time—a team should be able to function totally autonomously if a leader is doing their job right—it's just that the leader *is* there.

I first learned that lesson from my children. I found it was far easier to get them to do the washing up, not by yelling at them, but by getting off my butt and taking a "come on, let's do it" approach. Let *us* do it! Doing what we had to do ... together.

My team learned through me putting my attitude into action, if I could attend functions like these, then I would attend. However, if I couldn't be there for whatever reason, then they knew that my reason for not attending was genuine, and that I would want to be there supporting them. So, knowing this, they would still carry out the task at hand.

I used that same principle when we were implementing a new marketing strategy—one which proved successful in helping my team capture a $1,000,000,000 market share for our company. Yes, that's a billion dollars!

Our team were often required to attend various seminars and give short presentations during these events. The standard practice in other states was for the speaker to arrive 10 to 15 minutes before they were due to speak and to leave a few minutes after talking. These speakers would leave behind a handful of information flyers that potential customers were supposed to pick up, take with them and hopefully act upon.

My team took a more assertive approach. We would arrive 20 to 30 minutes before the seminar actually started, welcome guests, and make certain that our brochures were handed to everyone who attended as they entered the seminar (something to read while they waited for the seminar to start). We were also there for the coffee break and for 10 to 20 minutes after the seminar finished, just in case there were any questions. It was a far bigger commitment to the old way of doing things in time, effort and manpower. But the results were worth it. We certainly gained a lot of appointments that way and came to dominate our marketplace, unlike the rest of the state offices.

In the beginning I attended every function, doing what I wanted my team to do. To me it was all about leading from the front; leading by example. Did I *have* to turn up to do this? No. My team were more than capable of doing it on their own—and they even improved on what I wanted. However, by being there I was able to take a hands on, team approach.

I may have been their leader, but if it was good enough for them then it was good enough for me.

I didn't just demand that they do it the way I wanted it done. I went with them and did what they had to do alongside them until they saw for themselves how successful this new approach was. If required I would be there first and I would be there last.

Case study - Bob Ansett and Niki Lauda

The Ansett name is legendary in Australian business circles. Sir Reginald Ansett established Ansett Airways in 1935. His son, Bob, established and led Budget Rentals which became a highly successful car rental company in the 1980s.

Bob wasn't a man to sit in the background leading his business from the comfort and safety of the boardroom. He was a man who led by example and expected his leadership team to do the same.

He expected his leaders to understand the issues their teams faced and had every manager, including himself, spend at least one day a month in a face-to-face customer contact role. This was his way of ensuring that his leaders stayed in touch with what was happening several layers removed from their everyday function in running a major corporation. It was a day when the leaders could talk to their team and find out what was really happening at the coalface.

Niki Lauda, the former Formula 1 racing car driver and founder of Lauda Air, took a similar approach. He would often buy a ticket on his own airline just to talk to his staff and passengers, to experience what they did when flying with his company. It was an important way for him to keep in touch with the people who made his company successful.

History is littered with so-called leaders who stayed away from the frontline and lost in the end. They lost because they relied on second, third and fourth-hand information and had no personal experience or understanding of what was really happening at the business end of the battles their people were fighting. The result of this method of leadership is usually rampant misinformation and acts of self-preservation by those who aren't performing.

Look at how effective this approach was for the old Communist state of the USSR. Here the Politburo was led to believe, year after year, that there was yet another record crop waiting to be harvested as in all previous years—when the crops were actually failing. This approach certainly worked for them didn't it?

How many managers deliberately place themselves in a similar position and wonder why things go wrong? How many managers don't put themselves on the frontline with their team? How many managers rely on their team to do the things which they aren't willing to do themselves? How many pretend leaders sit in the background being 'pushers' rather than real leaders? How many leaders of people are last to arrive and first to leave?

Far too many! And pity the people who work for them.

Sure, a Values Inspired Leader may not be able to do the tasks as well as those they lead, but that shouldn't stop them from getting out and mixing it with their team. Not in some glorified "I feel good doing this for you" team building exercise whose relevance is lost over a few beers later that night; but in the real world in which the team works.

They see what the team sees.

They face what the team have to face.

They are willing to work harder and longer than the team if required.

They work with the team together as they all strive for success.

They never take the position that they are superior to anyone in the team—they are just the leader of the team; a Leader who is equal to each of the team members.

They show a "let us" attitude.

They lead, and do not push.

Through it all, the Values Inspired Leader never loses contact with the one quality that defines them as a Leader who cares—being human.

Questions for Values Inspired Leaders

25 Am I a Leader or a Pusher?

26 Am I the first to arrive and the last to leave?

27 Do I ask the team to do things I'm not willing to do myself, or do I lead by example?

28 How can I better show this quality to my team?

100

Lesson 8

Be human

– Lesson 8 –

Be human

Some years ago I worked for a manager who would never say, "Good Morning" to his staff. Every day he would walk past us and ignore us. However, we were expected to greet him. Know any managers like that?

What is it? Is there some law of management that says when you become a leader of people you are to give up your good manners and humanity? Is there something that states that managers are superior to everyone beneath them—or must they just view everyone as being beneath them? Is there a rule that says that the workplace can't be fun and an enjoyable place to be?

Because if there is, then I missed that lesson—and would certainly be guilty of breaking every one of those rules! It is sad to see that so many workplaces have less life in them than a morgue. How can people stand to work there?

A Values Inspired Leader recognises the importance of their team's work environment. They recognise that an enjoyable place to work is just that, an enjoyable place to work. A place where people don't mind being 8 hours a day, 5 days a week, 48 weeks a year, for 40 to 50 years of their life.

They understand the importance of celebrating special occasions and the impact that rewarding excellence has on the team. They understand that having a bit of fun at work does not detract from the professionalism of the workplace, rather that it adds to it.

They also understand that human beings build relationships of trust with other human beings who demonstrate their "humanity." A Values Inspired Leader recognises that they can be human in their approach *and* be friendly, without necessarily having to be a friend to the team members. You don't have to have a group love-in to show you care about your people. It is enough to just be friendly, open, honest, caring, trusting and down-to-earth.

In one leadership role I held, one of the most important times of my work day was about 10 minutes after start time—just after I said "Good morning" to everyone. That was when I made each team member a cup of coffee, delivered it to their desk, and spent a few seconds catching up with them individually.

In those few moments I could be made aware of any issues that might have arisen or about special events on that day. These were the most valuable 15 minutes of my day and beat any one-hour long team meetings I could ever hold. Not only did I communicate with my people, I also showed how much I respected them and their work.

Another important "meeting" time was morning tea; when most of the team, including those from the field who happened to be in the office at the time, would sit around the table and have a coffee together. I wasn't a boss during these breaks, just another member of the team. In that time, we discussed everything from politics to sport to fashion to personal issues – just as any group of friends would at any café.

Many a time I received an informal 'heads-up,' a warning, on potential issues that could then be dealt with quickly and quietly. The success of those coffee breaks can never be underestimated.

Now, that is what worked for me with my teams. What would work for you in your environment as the Values Inspired Leader of your team? What can you do each day in order to keep in touch with your team members and stay human?

No, sending a daily email or weekly newsletter does not constitute keeping in touch! I am talking about face-to-face, human interaction.

Case Study - A leader's humanity on display

For me, the best lesson about the importance of being human in our approach to those who serve us, comes from The Bible. Christ, the leader of His disciples, often displayed His humanity and the understanding He had for His people, by performing some act of caring for them.

A perfect example of this was when He washed the feet of His disciples. At that moment He placed himself as a servant to His followers. The Master became the servant. He showed by His humanity that He was one with them and not above them—despite the position He held amongst them.

We don't have to wash the feet of our team members. Values Inspired Leaders just have to show that they are human and one with their people—not one above them.

Humans talk to each other.

Humans show emotions.

Humans form relationships.

Humans turn to people they trust when in crisis.

Humans want to feel they belong, that they are listened to and that someone does care.

They also like to have fun.

Case Study - A case for laughter and fun

David E was one of the best people I have ever had under my leadership. At the time I was a National Training Manager and David was my assistant.

Other than being involved in training, David and I had one thing in common; we believed in having fun. In fact, those outside of our department often thought that that was all we did—have fun. I know that because I was often questioned about it by other managers!

What they saw and heard were those few seconds every now and again when David and I would have a laugh, share a joke or make one-line comments to each other; and woe betide anyone who walked into our department!

What they didn't see were the long hours and the weekend workdays when he and I worked against tight deadlines to co-ordinate the gathering of information from other departments, to write the training manuals, and to plan the delivery of the training material for a company that had offices in every state across the country. In one six-week period I can recall us spending only six nights at our own homes. The rest of the time we were either travelling or in the office working.

Having fun kept us sane. Having a laugh made the pressure bearable. Making the workplace enjoyable made us more productive. Having fun was frowned upon, but I wouldn't have changed a thing.

The *Readers Digest* have a section in their magazine called *Laughter, The Best Medicine*. And it is! Illnesses have reportedly been cured through laughter. The endorphins released by laughter make us feel good; they put us on a natural high for a short time.

"Patch" Adams, the doctor made more famous by the movie of that name, even opened a hospital, called *The Gesundheit Institute*, which has a serious focus on laughter and fun in the treatment of illness. There are even "laughter clubs" starting all around the world that meet every morning so that people can start their day with a rollicking good laugh.

Let's face it, who said work has to be dull and boring? Can you imagine how depressing some workplaces must be—and for far too many people they are —simply because there is so little fun in the workplace or so little place for being nice; for being human.

Values Inspired Leaders show their humanity by being willing to allow and have a *bit* of fun. They encourage the workplace to be an enjoyable place; after all people will spend up to a third of their adult life at work.

Values Inspired Leaders will celebrate special events, such as birthdays and successes. One team I worked with even cooked a Christmas Dinner in the office and everyone came to that lunch—all during work hours.

There are times where I even put on events that my team's partners could also attend. As I saw it, they were a part of our success as well. Too often companies forget that partners share in the cost of each of their successes. So why shouldn't a company recognise them also? Overall it didn't cost that much. In fact, I saw it as an investment rather than a cost. It was my way of saying "thank you".

Values Inspired Leaders can never afford to lose or stop displaying their humanity. They understand that displaying a "human" side to their actions in no way diminishes either their status as a leader or their capacity to lead. In fact, they know that it enhances them.

Values Inspired Leaders who are in touch with their humanity also recognise that they are not gods; hiding their emotions and feelings. They recognise that they *do* have emotions and issues that they have to deal with and that they do not have to carry the burden on their own. They realise that at times they need someone they can trust and talk to in confidence.

Values Inspired Leaders are never afraid to admit that on occasion they themselves need help and guidance.

Values Inspired Leaders are always willing to seek counsel in what they do, without ever conceding responsibility for their actions.

Questions for Values Inspired Leaders

29 How do I show myself as being "human"?

30 How do I make the environment my team operates in one that they feel they want to work in?

– Lesson 9 –

*A leader seeks counsel,
and accepts responsibility*

– Lesson 9 –

A leader seeks counsel, and accepts responsibility

"The Buck stops here!"

Never has there been a more apt definition of the responsibility of leadership.

Made by American President Harry Truman, it is an oft quoted reference to the loneliness that comes with leadership. At the end of the day a leader—be they in business, politics or society—is responsible for whatever happens under their leadership.

Sure, some people under the leader may stuff-up and perform in a way that diminishes the results of the team. Sure, the opposition may do something that affects outcomes, or head-office fails to deliver on its promises, or you are forced to take actions that go against your advice, or any one of a thousand other things may arise that prevent us from achieving the results we want.

So, what

People can make all the excuses they want, but in the end the buck stops at the desk of the leader.

A Values Inspired Leader is willing to share the successes of their team with the team. Yet they are also willing to take sole responsibility for their team not succeeding or having done something wrong. It's not an easy thing to do. Then again, have I said anywhere that being a Values Inspired Leader is easy?

What makes a Values Inspired Leader the outstanding leader they should be is this: taking responsibility for what doesn't work out as it should and looking for solutions to the things that have gone wrong.

They won't waste time and energy looking for someone to blame. Values Inspired Leaders prefer to spend their time looking for solutions and determining the corrective actions that they will need to take. They show they are willing to shield their team members from the repercussions of failing to gain the required result.

Does that mean that the Values Inspired Leader allows the team to get away from all responsibility? No! The Values Inspired leader knows that they are accountable for the success or otherwise of both their team and the individual team members.

If a manager...

- seeks to blame everyone and everything for those matters that don't work out;
- lies to protect themselves;
- fails to acknowledge their mastery over a situation;

- fails to look for solutions because they are too concerned with denying their responsibility for a situation;

… then so will the team.

In other words, the leader will end up with a team that is always blaming someone else and which never looks at how they can improve their *own* performance. They live in a world of denial.

The Leader who is accountable and accepts responsibility for a situation, is one who develops within their team that same sense of accountability and responsibility. They develop a team that is willing to look at their own actions and take corrective action without seeking blame.

The example of the leader determines the performance of a team.

Importantly, by taking responsibility and being accountable for all that happens within their team, the Values Inspired Leader is able to set aside their own ego and seek counsel where required. They are secure enough in who they are as a leader and are not afraid to share the problems they face with someone they trust.

Case Studies - Harry Trumann, Walt Disney, Australia II

Could you imagine being in a position where your every decision could directly affect the lives of millions of people who look to you for leadership? That is exactly what leaders of countries face every day they are in power.

In the closing days of World War II, President Franklin D. Roosevelt had died and Truman, the Vice President, became the 33rd President of the United States of America. World War II was a conflict in which no country, no people were spared. It was to Truman that responsibility fell for approving the dropping of the two atomic bombs on Japan.

It was under that pressure that President Truman placed the plaque on his desk with the words, *"The Buck Stops Here"*. It was a constant reminder of the responsibility he carried as a leader. He knew he had to make tough decisions. He knew he had to make dramatic changes. He knew that history would judge him and he knew the lives of everyone who looked to him for leadership would be affected by his decisions. It was a terrible responsibility.

But who of us believes that he acted alone without seeking counsel from those he trusted? In fact, any President, past or present, probably seeks counsel from advisors who have advisors to their advisors. But who does the nation blame when things go wrong? Do they blame the researcher who provided the advisor with the information they gave to the President? No! They blame the President; they blame the leader as do people from all walks of life in their everyday lives.

We wouldn't expect a President or a Prime Minister to make major decisions without first seeking counsel. So why would we expect a Values Inspired Leader not to do the same thing? We shouldn't! A Values Inspired Leader understands the importance of seeking appropriate counsel in their decision making.

They also understand that with responsibility comes a great burden. They recognise that sometimes that burden is too much for any one person to carry alone. This is why great leaders have someone who is their personal counsel; someone they can unburden themselves with even if only for a short time. Every great leader has someone special like that in their life.

Walt Disney is someone who also sought counsel prior to making major decisions. However, his approach was somewhat different to the norm. It is said that Walt Disney would present his ideas to a group of 10 advisors and, if the majority of them rejected it, then he knew he had a good idea. Look at how well he did with Disneyland!

What this shows is that we don't have to agree with the people from whom we seek advice. It demonstrates the importance of seeking out the right type of counsellors; people who are willing to disagree with you or to state their own point of view. A Values Inspired Leader does not seek out the opinions of "Yes" people; those who always agree with them regardless.

The Values Inspired Leader receives points of view and ideas, or hears of issues they may never have thought about, through having counsel that is independent or free to speak its mind.

The Values Inspired Leader is also willing to accept that they may not be right all the time (heaven forbid!).

A Word on 'always being right.'

Have you ever worked in an organisation where it appeared as if the primary purpose of everyone was to simply please those in power by agreeing with the near divinity of their ideas, even when everyone other than those in power knew they were not the right ideas for success? Nobody dare speak out against the Big Boss's ideas, especially if they wanted to keep their job or be promoted!

We have all probably seen major strategies diluted to the point of failure simply to keep the boss happy. Some managers seem to believe that the only right ideas are their ideas – and when those ideas fail, then it wasn't the idea that was wrong, it's the fault of the people. Or just as effectively, they are never spoken of again.

I'd rather be The Values Inspired Leader who is successfully wrong, than a manager who is disastrously right. In other words, I'd rather take wise counsel that shows I am wrong and shows how success can be achieved, rather than ignoring that counsel simply because I am determined that *my* idea is *the* right idea. Just because a leader accepts responsibility for the success of an organisation doesn't mean that their ideas are the only right ones.

A great leader will take that counsel and weigh-up all the cases presented to them along with the information they already knew. Then they will make a decision by which they, as leader, will either sink or swim. They seek counsel but accept responsibility.

Sometimes the counsel the leader seeks is from the team itself. The story of *Australia II*'s 1983 America's Cup challenge is entrenched in the nation's sporting folklore. The New York Yacht

Club had held onto the Cup throughout 132 years of racing and it looked like that was the way it was going to stay. Nevertheless—even when the American team were leading three races to one, and needing just one more victory to retain the Cup—the *Australia II* crew and their skipper, John Bertrand, believed they could still win the next three races they needed to win.

The leadership team of Bertrand, Hugh Treharne (Tactician), Ben Lexcen (Designer) and Alan Bond (Syndicate owner), met constantly to plan their strategy, and to look for solutions. They turned to their crew for advice and assistance. These leaders weren't too proud to include their team in the decision-making process. *Australia II* did win that series and the America's Cup. It was a victory not of an individual, but of a team.

Sometimes the best counsel a leader can seek is from those who work directly for them, after all the team also have some interest in being the best they can be. Nevertheless, in this case the counsel should be limited to problem solving and seeking solutions, not for seeking advice about problems with other staff or managers. Those types of problems are best dealt with by outside or independent counsel.

It takes a person with the character of a Values Inspired Leader to stand up and declare that they are responsible when things go wrong. One only needs to look around them to see that lack of character being displayed. People from all walks of life can be seen trying to abrogate responsibility for their poor choices. It is as if someone else is always to blame for things that go wrong. Personal responsibility, it seems, has, like Elvis, left the building.

Often all levels of management seem only too quick to seek out someone else to blame when things go wrong, or to otherwise look to diminish their own responsibility for failure. Yet, this same management will act swiftly to garner glory for things that succeed.

It's hard to expect the youth of our nation to grow up with a sense of personal responsibility when so many of our business, community and national leaders appear to lack the integrity and courage required to be accountable and to take personal responsibility for the actions of both themselves and those who work for them. The example our leaders set, is the example our people will follow.

Values Inspired Leaders do not take the easy path. They take the honourable path. That doesn't mean a Values Inspired Leader has to resign every time something goes wrong or the expected results aren't achieved. It *does* mean that a Values Inspired Leader takes responsibility for what happens within their team and then acts to correct the aberration. They shield their team but work with their staff to ensure the mistakes don't continue.

A Values Inspired Leader seeks counsel but never abdicates responsibility to that counsel.

A Values Inspired Leader will take responsibility only for those things for which they are responsible. However, they will stand against accepting any blame cast onto their team for things that were the responsibility of persons outside that team. A true leader is not a doormat to be walked over; they will protect their team while helping them to be accountable too.

Values Inspired Leaders are the foundation upon which great teams are built and, like any foundation, they carry on their shoulders a great weight; a weight that at times they will feel they are carrying alone. Which is why they seek counsel.

A Values Inspired Leader needs to have integrity.

They need to be honest.

They need to be compassionate.

They need to be open and frank.

They need to be willing to carry a burden, seeking support not from their team but from a trusted counsel.

Values Inspired Leaders need to take responsibility for their actions. A Values Inspired Leader doesn't need to show they are right all of the time – they know they just need to get it right.

Again, the Values Inspired Leader needs to be seen as a Leader, not a 'Pusher'. The Values Inspired Leader gives their team a reason to follow them.

The Values Inspired Leader needs to be seen as a visionary, someone who people will *want* to follow; someone who can sell that vision to their team.

Importantly, they need to be a Leader who lives and breathes that vision; a Leader who is a part of the vision and someone who will take responsibility to make it happen.

Questions for Values Inspired Leaders

31 From whom do I seek counsel?

32 How do I manage my own stressful situations and help myself to be the best I can be?

33 How do I help my team in being accountable and in taking responsibility?

- Lesson 10 -

*A leader
needs more than a vision;
a leader needs
to be a part of the vision*

– Lesson 10 –

A leader needs more than a vision; a leader needs to be a part of the vision

Some years back I read one of the most magnificent mission/vision statements I have ever read. After several weeks of consultancy and coaching to the company, I approached the owner and congratulated him on such a wonderful vision. He was nearly bursting with pride—until I asked him when he thought he would actually put it into action.

Companies can spend tens of thousands of dollars developing a vision statement for their company; which is a complete waste of money for some. Others have an idea of what they want to achieve but can never find a way to put it into words. Finally, there are some who have no vision whatsoever; as far as they are concerned they have a business to run and are too busy to worry about that sort of nonsense.

Very few companies have an active vision—one where there are not just words on paper but where the organisation works toward the vision through every action each and every day.

It is said that without vision the people will perish. An even more profound statement is one made by Helen Keller, who said that the one thing worse than not being able to see is the person who has the ability to see, but who has no vision.

A vision gives the team focus. It tells them where they are headed. A well written vision will create enthusiasm for an ideal and give integrity to what the team does.

How can a team be expected to head in a certain direction if they don't know where they are expected to end up? If they don't know where they are going, then they could set off on a totally different tangent and yet still think they are on the right track.

Now, if they did end up in the wrong place, that wouldn't be due to any fault on the part of the team. It would be due to a failure on the part of a leader who has failed to lead. This is what happens when a manager expects their team to know where they should be going without any direction. The team has to know the vision so that they can recognise it when they get there, or so that they can realise they are going off course and alter direction.

Not only does a vision give direction it also sets the standards by which that journey is achieved. After all, how can any team be expected to achieve high standards if those standards have not been made crystal clear?

Everyone has their own expectation of what is an excellent product or standard of service delivery. Someone who has never had a good service experience will be blown away by some mediocre service delivery, while someone who only ever shops at the highest rated boutiques would be appalled by that very same service.

It's all a matter of perspective and expectations.

So how can any manager blame their team for not delivering work to the standards that the manager expects, if they have been given no guidance as to what those standards actually are?

How can any leader expect their team to be motivated to exceed expectations, to strive for excellence, and to keep giving their all when times get tough, if they have been given no vision or reason on why they should. (No, threatening someone with their job is not an approach a Values Inspired Leader takes).

A simple vision statement such as, "Our vision is to provide every customer with a superior and outstanding service experience," sets the tone for every aspect of the team's dealings with customers.
A vision allows the leader to ask the team, "How do we make this vision a reality in everything that we do, and how does it continuously redefine us as the market leaders in service and product delivery?"

When a vision is developed by a team it is owned by the team— but only as far as the leader takes ownership of that vision.

A team will look to their Values Inspired Leader for directions on the path to success.

Values Inspired Leaders realise the importance a vision holds for their team and they understand the importance of communicating that vision to them. They also recognise that if it is to be as effective as possible, then they need to be a part of the vision themselves. They have to become the catalyst for success.

The Values Inspired Leader knows that they need to live and breathe the vision if they are to have any chance of getting their team to work toward making that vision a reality.

A Word on a Leader's example

Leaders are watched and then judged by the examples they set. A Values Inspired Leader recognises that team members will only do a fraction of what the leader does.

- Show 100% commitment and chances are your team will return an 80% commitment.
- Show 80% and more than likely your team will give you a return of about 50-60%.
- Show 60% commitment and your team probably won't even bother turning up.

Treat your vision with disrespect and your team will show it utter contempt. It will be a vision that obviously has no meaning.

Far too many managers expect, or demand, that their team work towards making their vision a reality when they show themselves to be hypocrites by doing little on their own part towards making the vision real.

It's like the manager who demands that staff only take a 30-minute lunch break while they take 2 hours themselves; or the manager who insists everyone needs to be on time, even early, but is always late themselves; or the manager who demands that customers be treated with utmost respect and then treats their own staff like pigs and speaks ill of their customers behind their backs.

A Values Inspired Leader isn't someone who sits back and directs others to do what they aren't willing to do themselves. They realise that their actions will speak louder than any words; written or said. They know that their team are waiting for them to set the highest of examples.

The Values Inspired Leader knows that *any* example they provide will become the benchmark by which the team judge their own individual performances.

Ergo: a leader who sets the highest standard will receive the best result; and a leader who sets a lowly example will receive a poor result.

Values Inspired Leaders are true to their vision. They show faith in the path they forge. They are consistent, enthusiastic and steady. They act on knowledge and refuse to panic.

Case Study – Panic the vision destroyer

Under pressure some managers are prone to panic; to run their business unit based on the way the wind blows at any given moment on any given day. You've probably worked for someone like this – the type of manager who wreaks havoc, creates chaos and has everyone else running around, taking their eye off their real targets, simply in response to a criticism or half-understood "problem".

Imagine it's very late Friday afternoon and almost everyone has gone home. You return to the office and your manager presents you with an "urgent" problem based on a half understood message that no-one had confirmed as accurate. Phone calls have already been made to people that have gone home, more phone calls are demanded to those same people – to get the information that was needed from people who weren't available or is stored on computers at work that no-one, other than those people being phoned, has access to. Meanwhile the manager is contacting his managers informing them of a possible, as at this time unconfirmed, problem.

That's exactly the situation I faced one Friday after some days away from the office. The outcome? Nobody was able to confirm exactly what the problem was. Nobody was available to provide any information about the perceived problem. And a lot of panic was created.

Strangely (of course there is no cynicism here), on Monday morning it was found that there was no actual problem; just a misunderstood message and that all of the panic had been over nothing. Sadly, while this was a relatively unimportant incident that had no lasting effect on our business unit's outcomes, there are managers who act just like this on issues that do.

When a manager panics it creates confusion. When a manager reacts to an issue that is not fully understood it causes a lot of additional, unnecessary activity and workplace stress. It takes everyone's eye off the main picture. It creates a lack of trust in a manager's ability to lead people.

Subordinates expect their leader to cope with issues in a positive manner. They expect their leader to be capable of responding to issues in a measured, confident manner and not like a chook with its head cut off! They want to know that the person who is leading them is someone they can trust in a crisis; someone who will maintain focus on their objective and lead them safely to it. In a battle zone such a leader saves lives. In the workplace such a leader achieves results which bring success – which is what every team really wants.

Panic does nothing for a team. A Values Inspired Leader uses their vision to provide them with guidance, to give a sounding board for direction. This vision gives the Values Inspired Leader stability; they know where they are going and how they will get there. They hold faith in a vision that inspires them; giving them something to follow in a calm, assured manner.

Importantly, Values Inspired Leaders have a vision that not only inspires themselves but also inspires others to follow.

A Values Inspired Leader is someone who walks on pathways that have never been walked before. They dare to go places and meet challenges never before experienced.

A Values Inspired Leader challenges people to heights they never thought themselves capable of climbing.

They inspire not just with words but with action.

Which is why the values the Values Inspired Leader incorporates into every aspect of their life is so important. The Values Inspired Leader *is* the example.

Sometimes, the world it seems goes a little bit crazy, and may not always inspire people to display or even understand *how* to display the values that make a real, positive difference in this world. The only example these people may have of all that is right, of things that are good is in you, the Values Inspired Leader!

Case Study - A vision: Martin Luther King, Jnr.
"I have a dream." Those words spoken in August 1963 set the tone of a vision that Martin Luther King Jnr. would never see come to fruition. However, his belief in his vision, the values he displayed and his willingness to act and live towards achieving it, continues to inspire later generations to also seek his dream.

Nobody could ever doubt Dr King's commitment to his dream—it cost him his life. His is *the* brilliant example of what a leader's commitment to a vision should be, his actions, his values in life, are a timeless demonstration of the nature of true leadership.

Thankfully, Values Inspired Leaders don't normally have to give their lives as payment for achieving their vision. They just have to live it.

They become the inspiration for the vision.

They establish the values that underpin that vision.

In the end, they *become* the vision.

Questions for Values Inspired Leaders

34   What is my vision?

35   How do I live my vision?

36   How does my team approach the vision?

37   What do we, the team, have to do in order to make this vision a reality?

38   What have I learned about myself as a Leader from the Ten Lessons?

39   How would I like to be a better Values Inspired Leader?

40   How am I going to become a better Values Inspired Leader?

– *A final word* –

- A final word -

Values Inspired Leaders!

They don't expect respect, they earn it.

They show respect.

They trust.

They work with the very best people and give each of them the opportunity to be even better. They want their team members to succeed and celebrate their people's successes when they do.

They serve their team and show strength of character by being willing to stand alone against popular belief.

They are willing to listen and can take criticism without unleashing retribution.

They have the courage to fight for what they believe is right and protect those who need protection.

They are willing to work longer, harder and more consistently than their team. They are willing to be the first to arrive and the last to leave. They are willing to be a member of a team that is working as a whole.

They never lose sight of their humanity: to laugh some, encourage some, have fun some, smile some, cry some and share some.

They are willing to seek counsel and feedback. They are willing to be flexible, to learn and to change where change is needed.

They are willing to take responsibility—to openly declare, "It was my decision." They accept that the buck stops with them.

And they have a vision. A vision to always be better, to strive for higher heights and to never accept mediocrity.

Values Inspired Leaders show us what we are capable of achieving and inspire us to get there. They understand that together *with* the team we can achieve anything.

A Values Inspired Leader has a responsibility to their business, their team and to themselves. Leading is never about managing. It is about showing *real* leadership.

"Men make history and not the other way around. In periods where there is no leadership, society stands still. Progress occurs when courageous, skilful leaders seize the opportunity to change things for the better." Harry S. Truman (1884 – 1972).

"The signs of outstanding leadership appear primarily among the followers. Are the followers reaching their potential? Are they learning? Serving? Do they achieve the required results? Do they change with grace? Manage conflict?" Max de Pree (1924 -).

"Leadership is not magnetic personality--that can just as well be a glib tongue. It is not 'making friends and influencing people'--that is flattery. Leadership is lifting a person's vision to higher sights, the raising of a person's performance to a higher standard, the

building of a personality beyond its normal limitations." Peter F Drucker (1909 – 2005).

What an awesome responsibility.

No Leader takes any action in this world that doesn't affect others.

A Values Inspired Leader recognises that what they do, and the example they set, will touch everyone in their community.

The community, those around us in our workplace "community", or our family "community" or the greater "community" that surrounds us, are wanting to look up to their Leaders. People want to follow those with vision and drive and values.

The effects of the examples we set as Values Inspired Leaders will last longer than any of us will live. Like a pebble thrown into a pond, we will send out ripples upon the surface of society.

Recently I was talking with City Engineers from across my home state and I heard the most remarkable of stories.

Now, if there is one thing you would be expecting your City Engineers to be doing, I doubt if it would be chasing butterflies. Fixing roads and services, yes! But big, burly engineers in safety boots chasing butterflies across hilltops?!?

But that is exactly what one group of City Engineers is doing.

Not far from where I live there is a colony of butterfly, a very special butterfly, a highly endangered butterfly that these said same City Engineers are working to save.

These butterflies only live on and within 10 meters of one particular type of bush that exists only above a certain altitude on the side of a mountain. What the engineers are doing is planting clusters of those bushes within 20 meters of each other; allowing the butterflies to live in their own domain and at the same time intermingle with other domains, strengthening the gene pool of all.

Here is where the situation gets really interesting. Before it becomes a beautiful butterfly, the butterfly starts life as a caterpillar. This caterpillar feeds on the bush, keeping it trimmed and preventing it from dying by becoming too large.

In the root system of the bush lives a colony of ants, a certain type of ant. Every night these ants collect the caterpillar and carry them into their nest where the caterpillar secretes a liquid that the ants then use to feed their young.

In the morning, those ants carry the caterpillar back onto the bushes, where the whole cycle begins anew.

Isn't that just amazing!?!

In one little corner of our world lives a perfect example of a complete symbiotic synthesis of relationships; all working together to create beautiful butterflies. I was so touched I adopted the butterfly as my business symbol.

It is the Values Inspired Leader that has the capacity to bring that community together as no-one else can.

At times, as a Values Inspired Leader, we are just like the ant, carrying those around us to safety, nurturing and sheltering them until they can once again be placed out on to the branches and continue to grow into the amazing person they were always meant to be.

But more often than not, the Values Inspired Leader stops being the ant and becomes the butterfly itself.

The Butterfly Effect.

There is a theory that you may have heard of called, the Butterfly Effect.

This theory proposes that when a butterfly flutters its wings the air molecules around those wings are disturbed and because they are disturbed it affects the other molecules around them and as such, through the flow on effect, the whole world, by that single flutter of a butterfly's wings, is changed.

The theory was derived from Professor Emeritus Edward Lorenz's (1917 – 2008) 1969 theoretical example of a hurricane's formation being contingent on whether or not a distant butterfly had fluttered its wings several weeks before.

In other words, the smallest, gentlest action that could ever be taken has the power to change this world forever.

Imagine what effect we must have when we, as Values Inspired Leaders take our values and by our actions, just like the butterfly that flutters its wings ever so gently, share them with those around us; those from our own world, whom we touch in our lives– in our domain.

Just like the molecules around a butterfly's wings, those affected by us will also affect those around them.

Like the movement of the butterfly's wings, when we treat another with respect we change the world forever.

When we look for our shared values we change the world forever.

When we carry the weight of our neighbour to safety we change the world forever.

When we reward and feed others …….

When we let others believe in the possibility of themselves ……..

When we lead by example …….

When we show our humanity ………

…….. we change the world forever!

As leaders in your industry, the question you need to ask is what do you value most – the bottom line or holding yourself accountable to a set of values?

That is a choice only you can make.... and live by.

In a little world on the side of a mountain a beautiful butterfly is born. And with the flutter of its tiny wings, the world is changed.

Just like that butterfly, you as the Values Inspired Leader with the subtle and gentle flutter of *your* wings will also change the world forever!

If we face any challenge today I would say it is this, *to become better Leaders, who are inspired by values, who can inspire others with our vision—and who can pass that vision and those values on to our youth.*

Have strength and let who you are as a Values Inspired Leader be the inspiration to those future generations.

40 Values Inspired Leader's Questions

1	Do I expect my team to respect me just because of the position I hold or because of what I do?
2	What have I done or what do I do to earn the respect of my team?
3	What do I need to do to earn the respect of my team?
4	What is it about each of my individual team members that I respect?
5	How do I show my respect to the team?
6	How do I show I trust my team members?
7	What am I good at?
8	What are my team members good at?
9	Does my team have all the skills and abilities I need it to have in order to achieve my business goals
10	What additional skills and abilities do I need in order to achieve my business goals?
11	How am I developing my people?
12	Who am I developing to take over from me?

13	How do I need to develop them in order to better prepare them to take over from me?
14	How am I flexible?
15	Does my team trust me, and can they talk openly with me?
16	Do I hold grudges or seek to get even with people when I am criticised or told the truth?
17	What is my Continuous Improvement Process?
18	Do I ensure I Praise in Public and Reproach in Private?
19	How do I support my team fully and ensure that everything is in place for them to achieve what I want them to achieve?
20	What do I need to do to improve the way I support my team?
21	How do I show I am willing to stand up for my team?
22	How do I prepare my arguments?
23	How do I deliver difficult news and do I sell the positives?
24	How do I stop myself from being subservient to my team?
25	Am I a Leader or a Pusher?
26	Am I the first to arrive and the last to leave?
27	Do I ask the team to do things I'm not willing to do myself, or do I lead by example?

28	How can I better show this quality to my team?
29	How do I show myself as being "human"?
30	How do I make the environment my team operates in one that they feel they *want* to work in?
31	From whom do I seek counsel?
32	How do I manage my own stressful situations and help myself to be the best I can be?
33	How do I help my team in taking accountability and responsibility?
34	What is my vision?
35	How do I live my vision?
36	How does my team approach the vision?
37	What do we, the team, have to do in order to make this vision a reality?
38	What have I learned about myself as a Leader from the Ten Lessons?
39	How would I like to be a better Values Inspired Leader?
40	How am I going to become a better Values Inspired Leader?

About the Author

With over 35 years' management, business, sales and customer service experience, Colin, the principal of Colin Emerson Speaker and **TODAY!** Seminars and Director of the Professional Speakers Group, is a specialist in helping people achieve excellence, personally and in business. Colin has been responsible for transforming the service standards in some of Australasia's largest companies.

As a keynote speaker, Colin has delivered over 1000 conference, seminar and workshop presentations for leading businesses, training institutions and government agencies and conducts speaker training workshops and on-going coaching services to other professional speakers and trainers and business leaders.

As a state manager for a major bank he led a high performing team that achieved the amazing growth of over $1,000,000,000 within three years.

Colin is also author of 'Living The Valued Life – How An Ant Ate An Elephant'. Based on the results of over 10 years' research and hundreds of workshop hours and client successes, 'Living The Valued Life' describes 'The Process Of Achievement' which gives a step—by—step approach that enables anyone to achieve the things in life that are of value to them. It gives people strategies that enable them to move day by day towards making changes in their lives and the results have been outstanding.

He believes that Values Inspired Leadership leads to outstanding results for business, for people, for community and in life itself.

www.colinemersonspeaker.com

www.ingramcontent.com/pod-product-compliance
Lightning Source LLC
Chambersburg PA
CBHW070243190526
45169CB00001B/290